SALINE DISTRICT LIBRARY

W9-BOF-562

JE916.751 Wyn
Wynaden, Jo.
Welcome to the Democratic
Republic of the Congo

WITHDRAWN

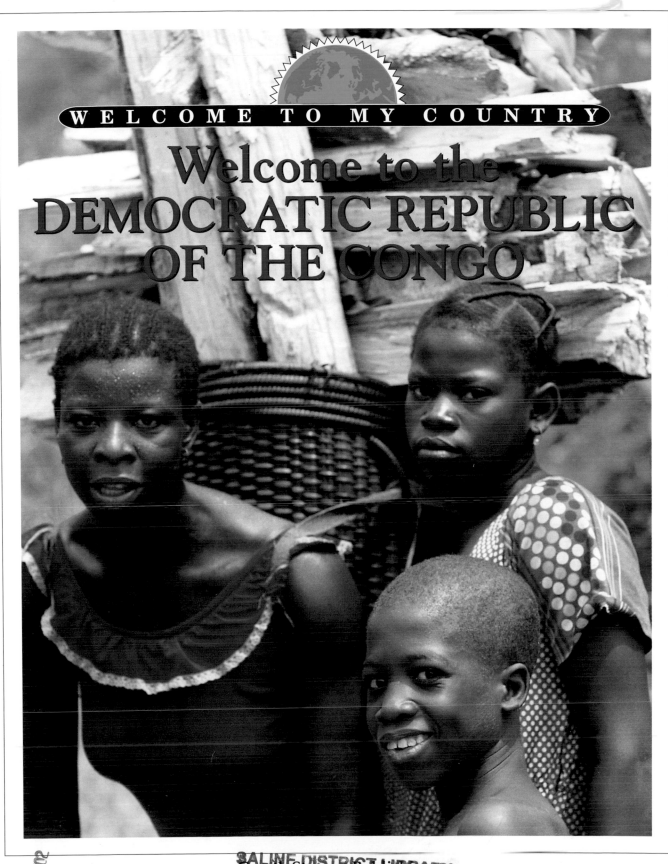

WELCOME TO MY COUNTRY

Welcome to the DEMOCRATIC REPUBLIC OF THE CONGO

SALINE DISTRICT LIBRARY
555 N. Maple Road
Saline, MI 48176

Gareth Stevens Publishing
A WORLD ALMANAC EDUCATION GROUP COMPANY

Written by
JO WYNADEN/NINA KUSHNER

Edited in USA by
DOROTHY L. GIBBS

Designed by
JAILANI BASARI

Picture research by
SUSAN JANE MANUEL

First published in North America in 2002 by
Gareth Stevens Publishing
A World Almanac Education Group Company
330 West Olive Street, Suite 100
Milwaukee, Wisconsin 53212 USA

Please visit our web site at:
www.garethstevens.com
For a free color catalog describing
Gareth Stevens' list of high-quality books
and multimedia programs, call
1-800-542-2595 (USA) or
1-800-461-9120 (CANADA).
Gareth Stevens Publishing's
Fax: (414) 332-3567.

All rights reserved. No parts of this book may be reproduced or
utilized in any form or by any means electronic or mechanical,
including photocopying, recording, or by an information storage and
retrieval system, without permission from the copyright owner.

© **TIMES MEDIA PRIVATE LIMITED 2002**
Originated and designed by
Times Editions
An imprint of Times Media Private Limited
A member of the Times Publishing Group
Times Centre, 1 New Industrial Road
Singapore 536196
http://www.timesone.com.sg/te

Library of Congress Cataloging-in-Publication Data
Wynaden, Jo.
Welcome to the Democratic Republic of the Congo / Jo Wynaden
and Nina Kushner.
p. cm. — (Welcome to my country)
Includes bibliographical references and index.
Summary: An overview of the country of the Democratic Republic of
the Congo which includes information on geography, history,
government, and social life and customs.
ISBN 0-8368-2530-6 (lib. bdg.)
1. Congo (Democratic Republic)—Juvenile literature. [1. Congo
(Democratic Republic).] I. Kushner, Nina. II. Title. III. Series.
DT644.W9 2002
967.51—dc21   2001042837

Printed in Malaysia

1 2 3 4 5 6 7 8 9 06 05 04 03 02

PICTURE CREDITS
Léonie Abo / University of Western
    Australia: 29
A.N.A. Press Agency: 7
ANACCO: 44
Archive Photos: 11, 37
Camera Press: 15 (both), 38
The Canadian Press Picture Archive: 14
    (David Guttenfelder), 16 (Blaise Musau),
    17 (Paul Chiasson)
Bruce Coleman Collection: 3 (center), 9
Dave G. Houser: 1
The Hutchison Library: 2, 3 (bottom), 5, 8,
    13, 19, 20, 21, 26, 35, 39
Björn Klingwall: 4, 27, 43
Charles D. Miller III: 36
North Wind Picture Archives: 10
Betty Press / Panos Pictures: 28
Marc Schlossman / Panos Pictures: 25, 33
Topham Picturepoint: 12, 40 (both)
Trip Photographic Library: Cover, 3 (top), 6,
    18, 22, 23, 24, 31, 32, 34, 41, 45

Digital Scanning by Superskill Graphics Pte Ltd

Contents

Words that appear in the glossary are printed in **boldface** type the first time they occur in the text.

4

Welcome to the Democratic Republic of the Congo!

The Democratic Republic of the Congo is a land of many cultures. Its capital is Kinshasa, and people commonly call the country Congo-Kinshasa. Let's find out more about this beautiful country!

Opposite: The Tutsis are one of many Congolese **ethnic** groups.

Below: Even on the street, Ping-Pong is a popular game in Congo-Kinshasa.

The Flag of the Democratic Republic of the Congo

The Congolese flag has a blue background with six small yellow stars running down the left side and one large yellow star in the center. This flag was adopted in 1997 by President Laurent Kabila.

The Land

Congo-Kinshasa, previously known as Zaire, is located in central Africa. Except for one short coastline to the west, along the Atlantic Ocean, it is bordered by nine other countries. With a land area of 905,564 square miles (2,345,410 square kilometers), Congo-Kinshasa is the third largest country in Africa.

Below:
Lush vegetation grows in Congo-Kinshasa's fertile soil, but only 3 percent of the country's land is used for farming.

Left: The Congo River runs across the cuvette. This low, flat land is covered with rain forests. *Cuvette* means "saucer" or "shallow bowl."

The Cuvette

The Congo River, one of the largest rivers in the world, flows through Congo-Kinshasa from the Katanga **plateau** to the Atlantic Ocean. About one-third of the country is the Congo Basin, or the *cuvette* (coo-VET).

Plateaus and mountains border the cuvette. The Ubangi-Uele plateaus are to the north. The Katanga plateau is to the south. The Mitumba, Virunga, and Ruwenzori mountains are in the east. The Crystal Mountains are in the west.

Climate

The cuvette is **humid**, with constant rainfall and temperatures of about 75° Fahrenheit (24° Celsius). Areas further west have less rainfall and are slightly warmer. Temperatures in the east are about 66° F (19° C).

The plateaus in the north and the south are cooler, but, because they are on opposite sides of the equator, they have opposite seasons. When the north is having its dry season, the south is having its rainy season.

Above: Corn grows very well in the rich **volcanic** soil of the Virunga Mountains.

Plants and Animals

Trees and a wide variety of other plants thrive in the rain forests of the cuvette. Many of these plants are used to make medicines. Congo-Kinshasa also has a variety of animals, from the lions and leopards on the grasslands to the crocodiles and hippos in the rivers. Due to hunters, however, the number of animals has decreased.

Left: Today, the animals of Congo-Kinshasa are protected by strict hunting rules.

History

Pygmies are believed to have been the very first people to live in the area that is now Congo-Kinshasa. Today, pygmies live in the Ituri Forest.

By the 1400s, the Bakongo people had moved into the region and had set up many separate kingdoms. One of the most important was the Kongo kingdom on the Atlantic coast.

The Portuguese arrived in 1482. They were the first Europeans to make contact with the people of the Kongo kingdom.

Left: Spanish navigator and mapmaker Juan de la Cosa drew this map in 1500. It shows Africa as it was known after Portuguese explorer Vasco da Gama sailed around the Cape of Good Hope, its southern tip, in 1497.

The Congo Free State

Belgium was the only European country to establish a **colony** in the Congo region. In the late 1800s, King Léopold II set up trading posts and made **treaties** with tribal chiefs. The Berlin West Africa Conference, held in 1884 to 1885, named Léopold the ruler of what he called the Congo Free State. In 1908, however, Belgium took away Léopold's power because of the cruel way he treated the people.

Above:
The Berlin West Africa Conference caused conflicts between African tribal groups. The Europeans who attended the conference divided Central and West Africa, splitting up kingdoms and forcing together tribal enemies.

Left: The joy of the Congolese over becoming independent did not last very long. The new republic was a true democracy for less than three months.

Independence

A new nation called the Republic of the Congo declared independence from Belgium on June 30, 1960, but the country was not ready to govern itself. The tribes would not cooperate with each other, and European leaders had left the country. Within weeks, violence between tribes and tension between President Joseph Kasavubu and Prime Minister Patrice Lumumba brought **democracy** to an end.

The Rule of Mobutu

Colonel Joseph Mobutu led a **coup** against Lumumba on September 14, 1960, and overthrew Kasavubu on November 25, 1965. After taking full control of the government, Mobutu ruled the Congo for thirty-two years.

Mobutu's government was **repressive** and dishonest. While he built a personal fortune that was worth billions, the Congolese grew poorer, and the country's economy collapsed.

Below: President Mobutu waves to supporters during an official parade in the early 1970s. Although he took power in 1965, Mobutu was not officially elected president until 1970.

Left: President Laurent Kabila changed the name of the country back to the Democratic Republic of the Congo. In 1971, President Mobutu had named it the Republic of Zaire.

Rebellion

In the 1990s, a continuing economic crisis within the country and growing problems with neighboring countries weakened Mobutu's power.

With support from the countries of Uganda, Rwanda, and Burundi, Congolese general Laurent Kabila led a **rebellion** against Mobutu. In May 1997, Kabila overthrew Mobutu and made himself president, but the unrest continued. In January 2001, Kabila was **assassinated**, and his son, Joseph Kabila, took control.

Immaculée Birhaheka (1958–)

A strong defender of human rights, Immaculée Birhaheka has worked for many years to inform Congolese women about their rights. At times, she has been beaten and arrested for speaking out against **prejudice**.

Joseph Kasavubu (c. 1913–1969)

In the 1950s, Joseph Kasavubu led the independence movement. In 1960, he became the first president of the Republic of the Congo. He was overthrown by Mobutu in 1965.

Joseph Kasavubu

Moise Kapenda Tshombe (1919–1969)

Moise Tshombe was the president of Katanga, a province that had separated from the Republic of the Congo in 1960. In 1963, Katanga rejoined the Republic. Tshombe fled to Spain but returned to serve as prime minister from 1964 to 1965.

Moise Kapenda Tshombe

Government and the Economy

After declaring independence from Belgium, Congo-Kinshasa was a struggling democracy until Mobutu seized power in 1965. As president, Mobutu turned the country into a **dictatorship**.

When Laurent Kabila overthrew Mobutu in 1997, he promised free elections and other political reforms. Instead, he postponed elections and took full control of the government.

Left: This tank is patroling a street in Kinshasa. Laurent Kabila ruled Congo-Kinshasa with a lot of help from the Congolese army.

Left: Although President Laurent Kabila (*center*) had put off elections in his own country, he took part in a conference on democracy with other world leaders in 1999.

Local Government

Congo-Kinshasa is divided into ten regions. All regions are controlled by the national government, but each region is run by a commissioner who is appointed by the president.

Every village in Congo-Kinshasa has a chief, who is usually a man, or a council of elders. The chief is either chosen by the villagers or **inherits** his position. The main duties of village leaders are to settle **disputes** and to ensure the well-being of the villagers.

The Economy

Copper was once the most important part of Congo-Kinshasa's economy. When copper prices dropped in 1974, the country's economy collapsed.

Before 1990, about 80 percent of Congo-Kinshasa's exports came from mining its rich mineral resources, such as diamonds, copper, platinum, gold, and silver. **Civil war**, however, has since reduced all exports, making the country even poorer.

Above: A woman harvests potatoes in the Virunga Mountains, north of Lake Kivu.

Agriculture

More than half the people in Congo-Kinshasa are farmers. Their main food products are sweet potatoes, **cassava**, peanuts, and vegetables. Most of the farmers grow food only for their own needs or for local markets because transporting crops on the country's poor roads and railroads is so difficult.

Mountains, forests, and the rainy seasons also make transportation in Congo-Kinshasa difficult. Not having good transportation is one of the main reasons the country remains poor.

Left: Although most Congolese travel from city to city by riverboat on the Congo River, some travel by train. Not one railroad, however, runs across the entire country.

People and Lifestyle

Ethnic Groups

The Congolese people represent more than two hundred ethnic groups, each with its own language and traditions.

The four largest groups make up about 45 percent of the country's population. They are the Mongo, the Luba, the Kongo, and the Mangbetu-Azande. The Pende, the Songe, and the Kuba peoples are some of the other larger ethnic groups.

Above: Villagers live simple lives without electricity or running water. They use oil lamps for light and get their water from nearby wells, springs, or rivers.

City Life and Country Life

The people living in Kinshasa, the country's largest city, are called *Kinois* (KEEN-wah). Most of them are very poor, yet they live side by side with the very rich.

More than half of the Congolese live in rural areas. Most of them are very poor. The civil war has destroyed homes and crops, and trade has been stopped in many places. Even in areas not affected by the civil war, people suffer from **malnutrition**.

Above: Many rural Congolese live in mud huts with roofs made out of **thatch**, grass, or palm leaves. The huts are cool in hot weather.

Education

Due mainly to the work of teaching **missionaries**, Congo-Kinshasa has one of the highest **literacy** rates in Africa. Schools run by the state often close when the economy is poor.

Although school is required up to grade six, many children do not attend because their parents cannot afford the fees for tuition, uniforms, books, and supplies. Sometimes parents need their children to help them with the family business.

Above: Congo-Kinshasa depends on the schools run by missionaries to provide most of the country's public education.

At the end of grade six, students take an examination to qualify for middle school. The two-year middle school program determines which students go on to high school and which can take **vocational training**.

Below: These students attend a post-high school institute. The institutes offer specialized study in law, business, nursing, teaching, or the arts.

High school graduates can enroll in a university or post-high school institute. Congo-Kinshasa has three state-run as well as several private universities. The country also has at least one post-high school institute in each district.

Religion

Congo-Kinshasa does not have an official religion, but 80 percent of its people are Catholics, Protestants, or Kimbanguists, who are followers of an African Christian church. Ten percent are Muslims. Others follow traditional beliefs, worshiping their ancestors and spirits of the natural world, such as tree or water spirits.

Above: Catholic worshipers wait outside a church to attend Mass. More than half of the Congolese are Roman Catholics.

Africanized Christianity

Most Christian churches in Congo-Kinshasa are Africanized, which means that church services reflect local cultures. Catholic services, for example, use local languages, and hymns are sung to African melodies and rhythms.

Some newer religions combine African roots and Christian traditions. The Kimbanguists are the largest new group. They reject magic and other traditional African practices.

Left: Arab and Swahili traders introduced Islam to Congo-Kinshasa in the nineteenth century. Today, most Congolese Muslims live in the eastern part of the country, separate from other groups. This mosque is in the Nord-Kivu region.

Language

The Congolese have more than two hundred languages and dialects. Four of them — Lingala, Swahili, Tshiluba, and Kikongo — have become the country's national languages. Lingala is the most common language spoken in the capital city of Kinshasa. French, however, is the official language of the government and the schools. After grade six, French is the only language spoken in the classroom.

Left:
Several French newspapers are sold on the streets of Kinshasa.

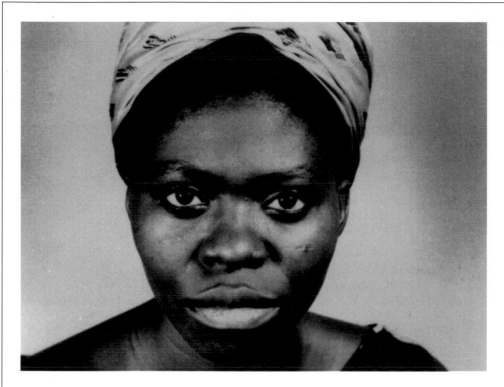

Left: Author Leonie Abo (1945–) caused a lot of excitement in 1991 with her autobiography, *Une Femme du Congo*, or *A Congolese Woman*. This book describes the violence during Mobutu's rule.

Literature

The literature of Congo-Kinshasa has developed only since the 1960s when Lovanium University, now University of Kinshasa, opened a literary center to help Congolese writers. Congolese authors often write about colonialism, tribalism, and conflicts between the modern and the traditional.

Famous Congolese writers include Philippe Lisembé Elebe (1937–), Clémentine Faik Nzuji (1944–), and Elisabeth Mweya Tol'ande (1947–).

Arts

Congo-Kinshasa is world famous for its ethnic art. The country's different ethnic groups make a variety of art forms, including beautiful cloth and dramatic masks, statues, and carvings.

Many pieces of Congolese art are **symbolic**. For example, when a Woyo woman marries, she receives pots with a **proverb** carved on each lid describing the relationship between a husband and wife. If she serves food to guests in a pot with a lid describing a husband mistreating his wife, her husband must discuss the problem with her, and guests can offer advice.

Congolese artwork can also have religious uses. Wedding and funeral rituals need masks and costumes, and statues are used in worship. Because artists are thought to be close to the forces of magic, some of their small religious sculptures, or fetishes, are believed to have special powers.

Right: This stool was made for a Luba chief. It is carved in the "long-face" style of the Luba-Henda people.

Music and Dance

Congolese love music. Rattles, bells, horns, drums, and the *kalimba* (kah-LIM-bah) are popular instruments. The kalimba is a wooden board with thin metal strips nailed to it. A person plucks the metal strips to play a tune.

Every religious ritual has its own music and dancing, with special tunes and rhythms.

Above: Children in Congo-Kinshasa make music with their bright yellow brass instruments.

Congolese musicians have created rumba dance music called *soukous* (SOO-koos). This music is a favorite all over Africa, and it is becoming popular even in Europe and America.

Left: These two women are dancing to soukous. This popular music developed when local bands added African melodies and rhythms to the Caribbean rumba. *Soukous* comes from *secouer* (SEH-coo-eh), a French word meaning "to shake."

Leisure

Children's Games

Most Congolese children make their own toys. Using **bamboo**, old boxes and tin cans, and worn-out tires, they can make wagons, scooters, and toy trucks. Boys usually play with these toys more than girls do. Girls most often play by imitating their mothers. A girl might tie a doll to her back and walk with her mother, who is carrying a baby the same way. This game trains girls to help care for younger children.

Below: Congolese children are proud of their homemade wooden scooters.

Pastimes

Singing and dancing are favorite pastimes for most Congolese. Rich villagers pay drummers to play for special occasions, such as the birth of a child or a good harvest. City people enjoy watching television, going to movies, or listening and dancing to soukous music.

Storytelling is an enjoyable tradition. Village storytellers usually recite folktales with a moral. In cities, stories are often about famous people.

Above: A disc jockey entertains people with the lively music of soukous bands.

Left: In turn, mankala players take all the stones from one of their pits and drop them, one at a time, into each pit to the right. If the last stone drops into an empty pit on the moving player's side of the board, that player can capture the stones in the pit directly across from it.

Mankala

A game called *mankala* (man-KAH-lah) is popular with both adults and children in Congo-Kinshasa. Mankala is played on a board that has fourteen cuplike pits, six along each side and one, called a "treasury," at each end.

A game begins with four stones, seeds, or beans in each pit along the sides. Players take turns moving their stones around the board, trying to capture each other's. The game is over when all the pits along one side are empty. The player who ends up with the most stones wins the game.

Sports

Soccer is Congo-Kinshasa's national sport. Boys often play it using a ball made of rags. Congolese also enjoy basketball, boxing, swimming, and riverboat racing.

Left: The Simbas, Congo-Kinshasa's national soccer team, won the African Nations Cup in 1974. Here, a Simbas player (*right*) battles for the ball during the 1998 African Nations Cup. Congo-Kinshasa beat Burkina Faso in the finals of that competition.

Holidays and Festivals

Independence Day, on June 30, which celebrates Congo-Kinshasa's 1960 break with Belgium, is the country's most important state holiday. The government holds parades to display its military strength on state holidays.

Left: Colorful celebrations take place throughout Congo-Kinshasa every year on Independence Day.

Other public holidays include the Christian holy days of Christmas Day, Easter Monday, and Ascension Day.

Traditional festivals in Congo-Kinshasa often honor ancestors or spirits, and some celebrate major life events, such as a boy's **initiation** to manhood. In the Bambuti (BAM-BOOT-ee) tribe of the Ituri Forest, boys are trained in hunting and other skills, then must pass physical tests.

Above: Initiation dances symbolize a boy's changing from child to adult.

Food

Congolese eat chicken and fish, but they sometimes eat monkey, wild lizard, and elephant, too. A favorite dish, *moambé* (MOH-am-bay), is chicken in a sauce made of tomatoes, peanut butter, ginger, oil, and pepper.

Above: Fish is a common part of the Congolese diet.

Left: This woman pounds cassava into a powder. To prepare cassava, she will mix some of the powder with water and cook it for several minutes.

Left: Mealie meal is cornmeal porridge that is made by mixing cornmeal and water. The mixture is stirred while it cooks, until it is almost solid.

Most meals in Congo-Kinshasa include rice, cassava, or manioc bread, which is made from cassava. These foods are always served with sauces. Many of the sauces are hot and spicy. Meat is expensive, so it is eaten only once a week or less.

At mealtime, rice, cassava, or bread is served in a big bowl. Family members gather around the bowl to eat. Diners eat with one hand, usually the right hand. They take handfuls of rice, cassava, or bread, mix in a little sauce, shape it into balls, and eat it.

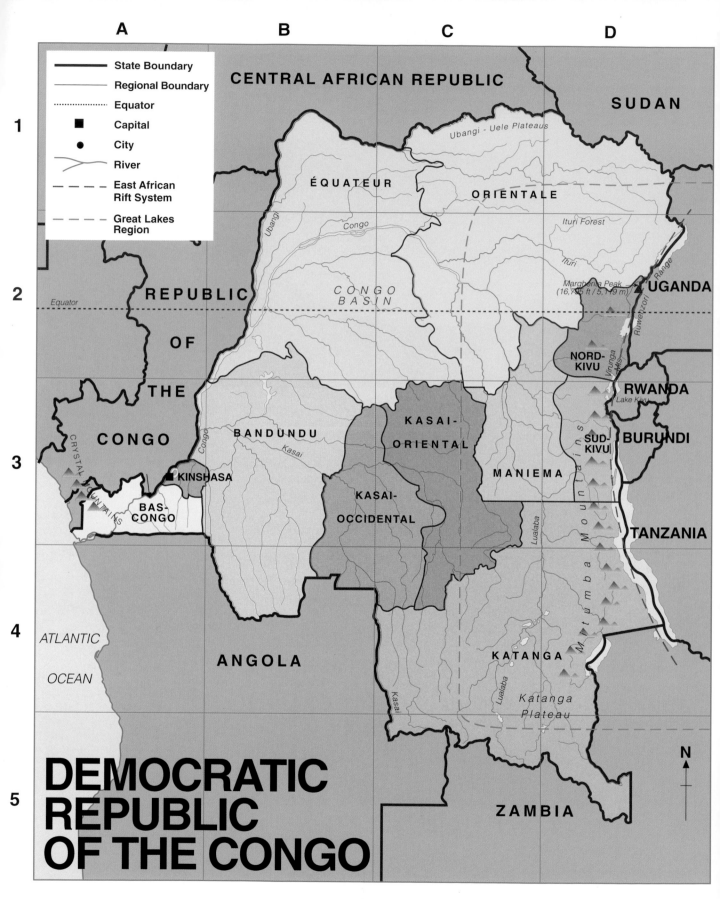

DEMOCRATIC REPUBLIC OF THE CONGO

Above: The Virunga Mountain range has active volcanoes and beautiful waterfalls.

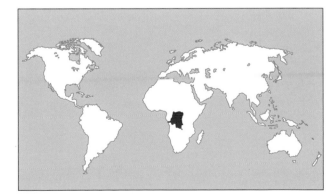

Quick Facts

Official Name	Democratic Republic of the Congo (since 1997)
Former Names	Republic of Zaire (1971–1997); Democratic Republic of the Congo (1964–1971); Republic of the Congo (1960–1964); Republic of the Belgian Congo (1908–1960); Congo Free State (1885–1908)
Capital	Kinshasa
Official Language	French
Population	51,964,999 (July 2000 estimate)
Land Area	905,564 square miles (2,345,410 square km)
Regions	Bandundu, Bas-Congo, Équateur, Kasai-Occidental, Kasai-Oriental, Katanga, Maniema, Nord-Kivu, Orientale, Sud-Kivu
Highest Point	Margherita Peak 16,795 feet (5,119 m)
Major Rivers	Congo, Kasai, Lualaba, Ubangi
Major Religions	Roman Catholic, Protestant, Kimbanguist, Islamic, traditional African religions
Main Tribes	Kongo, Luba, Mangbetu-Azande, Mongo
Currency	Congolese Franc (CF 47.26 = U.S. $1 in 2001)

Opposite: Congolese children sell souvenirs to tourists.

Glossary

assassinated: murdered, usually for political reasons.

bamboo: a kind of tropical grass with a tall, hollow, woody stem.

cassava: a tropical shrub with a starchy root that can be eaten in several ways.

civil war: a war between citizens of the same country.

colony: an area in one country that is controlled by another country.

coup: a sudden military action to take over a government.

democracy: a government in which the people rule themselves through their elected representatives.

dictatorship: a government ruled by one person who has all the power.

disputes: arguments or quarrels.

ethnic: related to a group of people from a particular country or culture.

humid: damp, usually describing the amount of moisture in the air.

inherits: receives objects, status, or qualities from a person, usually a relative, who has died.

initiation: the process of being admitted into a group or club, often after a test.

literacy: the ability to read and write.

malnutrition: poor health caused by not eating enough nutritious food.

missionaries: people belonging to a religious group who go to another country to teach, spread their religion, and do charitable work.

plateau: a wide area of high, flat land.

prejudice: a dislike for someone or something based on beliefs and opinions rather than on facts.

proverb: a wise and catchy saying that states a familiar truth.

pygmies: various tribes of African people who live in tropical regions and are unusually short in height.

rebellion: a fight against an authority.

repressive: not allowing people to act or speak freely.

symbolic: representing or standing for something else.

thatch: natural material, such as straw or leaves, used to cover a roof.

treaties: formal agreements between countries, often to settle disputes.

vocational training: a course of study and practice to learn the skills needed for a particular job.

volcanic: produced by or coming from a volcano.

More Books to Read

Africa. Continents series. Leila Merrell Foster (Heinemann Library)

The Art of African Masks: Exploring Cultural Traditions. Art around the World series. Carol Finley (Lerner)

Congo in Pictures. Visual Geography series. (Lerner)

Democratic Republic of the Congo. Cultures of the World series. Jay Heale (Marshall Cavendish)

Elizabeti's Doll. Stephanie Stuve-Bodeen (Lee & Low Books)

Exploration of Africa. Great Explorers series. Colin Hynson (Barron's Juveniles)

Kings and Queens of Central Africa. Sylviane Anna Diouf (Franklin Watts)

The Kongo Kingdom. African Civilizations series. Manuel Jordan (Franklin Watts)

Monkey Sunday: A Story from a Congolese Village. Sanna Stanley (Farrar, Straus & Giroux)

Mountain Mists: A Story of the Virungas. Evelyn Lee (The Nature Conservancy)

Videos

Hidden Congo: The Forest Primeval. (National Geographic)

Raft of Zaire. (Video Treasures)

Zaire: Tracks of a Gorilla. (Wildlife International)

Web Sites

home.iprimus.com.au/eddiema/ mancala/mancala.htm

www.cwu.edu/~yaegerl/ pygmypage.htm

www.infoplease.com/ipa/ A0198161.html

www.nationalgeographic.com/ congotrek360

Due to the dynamic nature of the Internet, some web sites stay current longer than others. To find additional web sites, use a reliable search engine with one or more of the following keywords to help you locate information about Congo-Kinshasa: *Congo River, Laurent Kabila, Kimbanguist, Kinshasa, mankala, Mobutu, Zaire.*

Index